MAR - - 2023

STARK LIBRARY

T4-ADM-058

DISCARD

POETRY POWER

QUATRAIN POEMS

By Ruthie Van Oosbree ✧ Poems by Lauren Kukla

Big Buddy Books

An Imprint of Abdo Publishing
abdobooks.com

abdobooks.com

Published by Abdo Publishing, a division of ABDO, PO Box 398166, Minneapolis, Minnesota 55439. Copyright © 2023 by Abdo Consulting Group, Inc. International copyrights reserved in all countries. No part of this book may be reproduced in any form without written permission from the publisher. Big Buddy Books™ is a trademark and logo of Abdo Publishing.

Printed in the United States of America, North Mankato, Minnesota
052022
092022

THIS BOOK CONTAINS RECYCLED MATERIALS

Design: Emily O'Malley, Mighty Media, Inc.
Production: Mighty Media, Inc.
Editor: Jessica Rusick
Cover Photograph: Chris Ryan/iStockphoto
Interior Photographs: Africa Studio/Shutterstock Images, p. 18; all_about_people/Shutterstock Images, p. 21 (boy); Aref Barahuie/Shutterstock Images, p. 5; blackCAT/iStockphoto, p. 11; Eric Isselee/Shutterstock Images, p. 14; EZ-Stock Studio/Shutterstock Images, p. 29; Fernando Astasio Avila/Shutterstock Images, p. 15 (moon); FG Trade/iStockphoto, p. 23; Inkley Studio/Shutterstock Images, p. 25 (Humpty Dumpty); Library of Congress, p. 7; Manatchon/Shutterstock Images, p. 15 (garbage can); Monkey Business Images/Shutterstock Images, p. 17; neelsky/Shutterstock Images, p. 13; pepan/Shutterstock Images, p. 25 (king); ShineCrazy/Shutterstock Images, p. 9; Steven Leon Day/Shutterstock Images, p. 19; triutamis/Shutterstock Images, p. 21 (star); Yobro10/iStockphoto, p. 27
Design Elements: mhatzapa/Shutterstock Images (paper doodles); Mighty Media, Inc. (backgrounds)

Library of Congress Control Number: 2021953300

Publisher's Cataloging-in-Publication Data
Names: Van Oosbree, Ruthie; Kukla, Lauren, authors.
Title: Quatrain poems / by Ruthie Van Oosbree and Lauren Kukla
Description: Minneapolis, Minnesota : Abdo Publishing, 2023 | Series: Poetry power | Includes online resources and index.
Identifiers: ISBN 9781532198960 (lib. bdg.) | ISBN 9781098272890 (ebook)
Subjects: LCSH: Poetry--Juvenile literature. | Poetry and children--Juvenile literature. | Quatrain--Juvenile literature. | Rhyme--Juvenile literature.
Classification: DDC 821.0--dc23

CONTENTS

Quatrains 4
Fitting the Form 8
Animal Quatrains 12
Sports Quatrains 16
Favorite Things Quatrains 20
Character Quatrains 22
Friendship Quatrains 26
Sharing Your Quatrain 28
Glossary 30
Online Resources 31
Index 32

QUATRAINS

A quatrain is four lines long. It can be an entire poem. It can also be a **stanza** in a longer poem.

Quatrains were first written in ancient times. They have been a common form of poetry for thousands of years. Quatrains are still published today.

Persian poet Omar Khayyam wrote famous quatrains in the 1000s and 1100s.

American poet Emily Dickinson was a famous quatrain writer. Dickinson lived in Massachusetts in the 1800s. She wrote almost 1,800 poems. Most were written with quatrain **stanzas**.

Emily Dickinson was known for writing poems with unique capitalization and punctuation.

FITTING THE FORM

Quatrains usually follow a **rhyme scheme**. Rhyme schemes are shown with letters. The letters represent the sound each line ends with. Lines that have the same letter **rhyme**. Common quatrain rhyme schemes are ABAB, AABB, and ABCB.

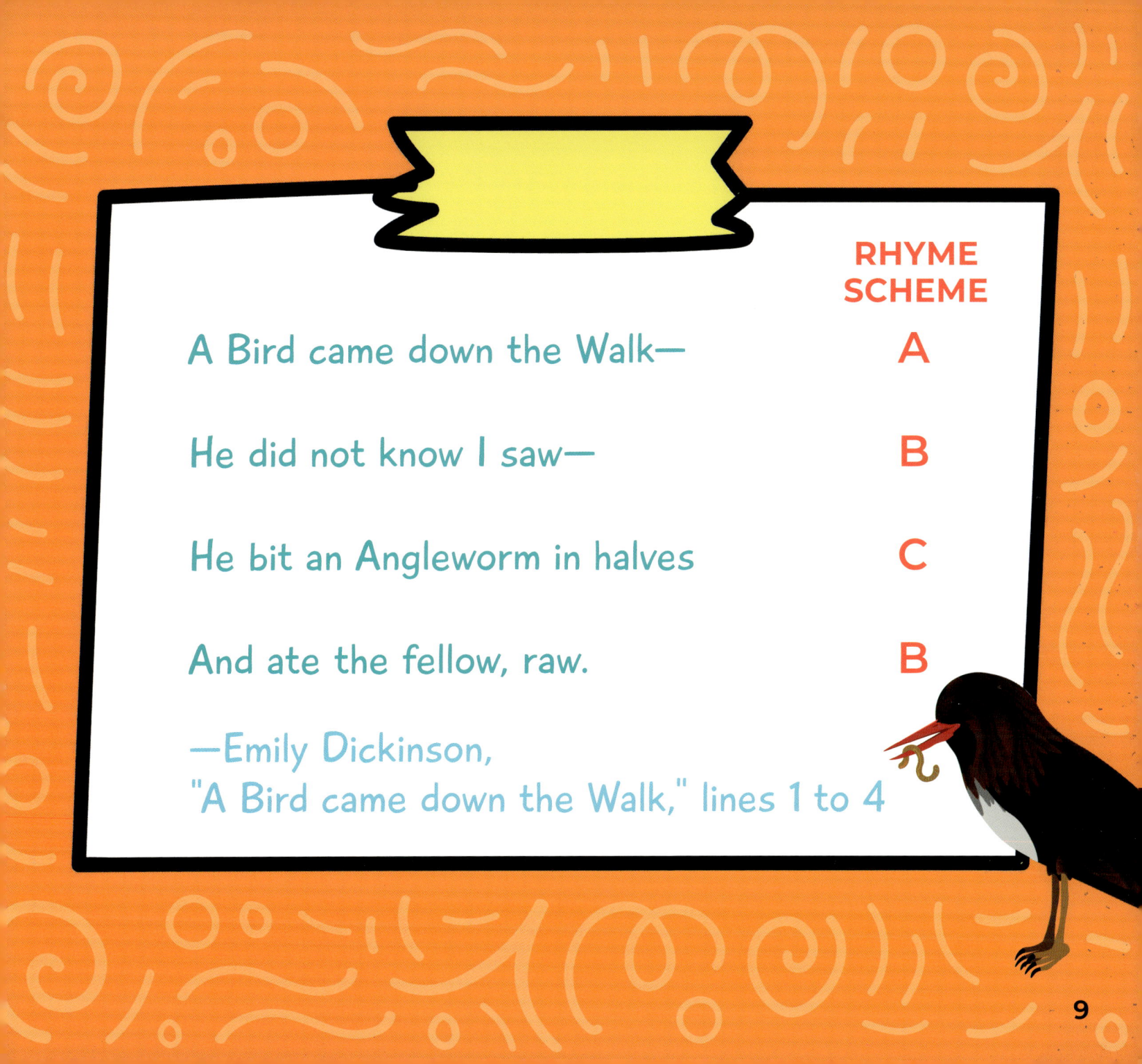

	RHYME SCHEME
A Bird came down the Walk—	A
He did not know I saw—	B
He bit an Angleworm in halves	C
And ate the fellow, raw.	B

—Emily Dickinson,
"A Bird came down the Walk," lines 1 to 4

A quatrain's lines can be any length. Some forms have a certain number of **syllables** per line. There may be ten syllables in each line. Or the lines may switch between eight and six syllables.

Read your poem aloud to help count the syllables.

ANIMAL QUATRAINS

Write a quatrain about an animal doing something interesting. Make a list of words that describe the animal. Write down things the animal does. Come up with **rhymes** for the words you've written.

TIPS & TRICKS
Use a rhyming dictionary if you can't think of a rhyme!

You can write your animal quatrain about a wild animal or a pet.

Tell a four-line story about the animal. End some lines with **rhyming** words.

You might pick a **rhyme scheme** right away. Then you can write lines to fit it. Or you might write many lines. Then you can choose some to fit a rhyme scheme.

At night beneath the shining moon

A raccoon walks the street

He looks in trash cans here and there

To find a treat to eat

What is this quatrain's rhyme scheme?

SPORTS QUATRAINS

Make a list of words related to your favorite sport. Add pieces of **equipment**. Write down action words, such as *kick* or *throw*. You could also list things that happen in the sport.

You could write about a game you played in.

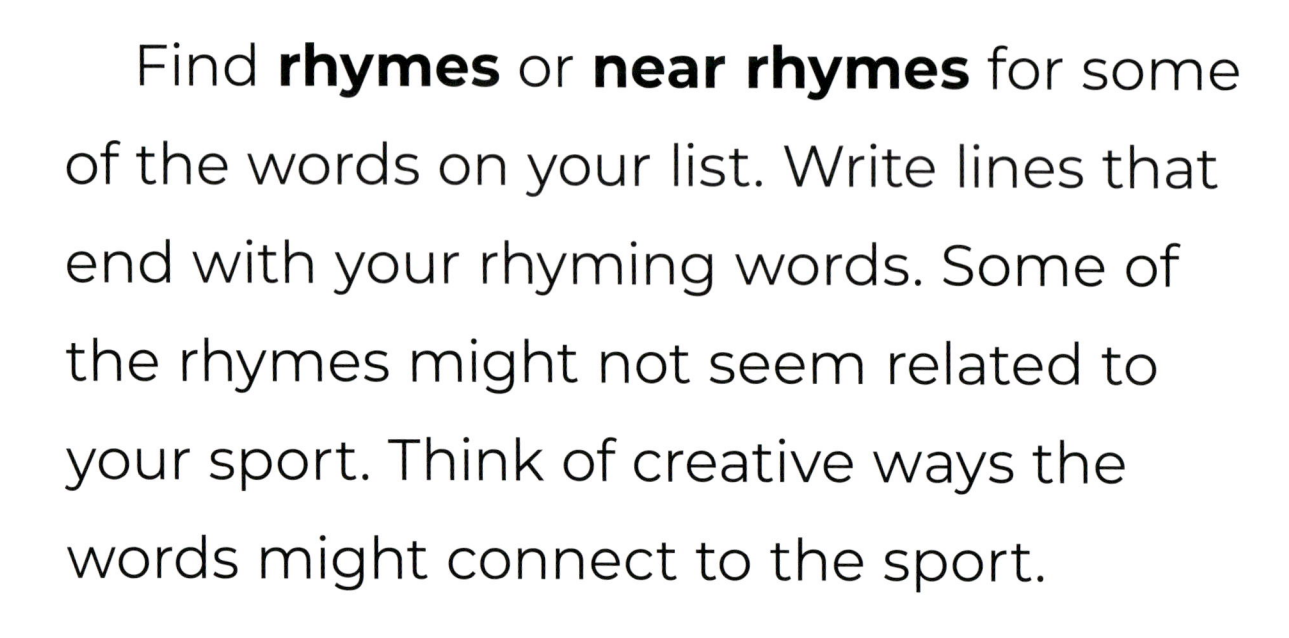

Find **rhymes** or **near rhymes** for some of the words on your list. Write lines that end with your rhyming words. Some of the rhymes might not seem related to your sport. Think of creative ways the words might connect to the sport.

Two strikes, three balls, three guys on base

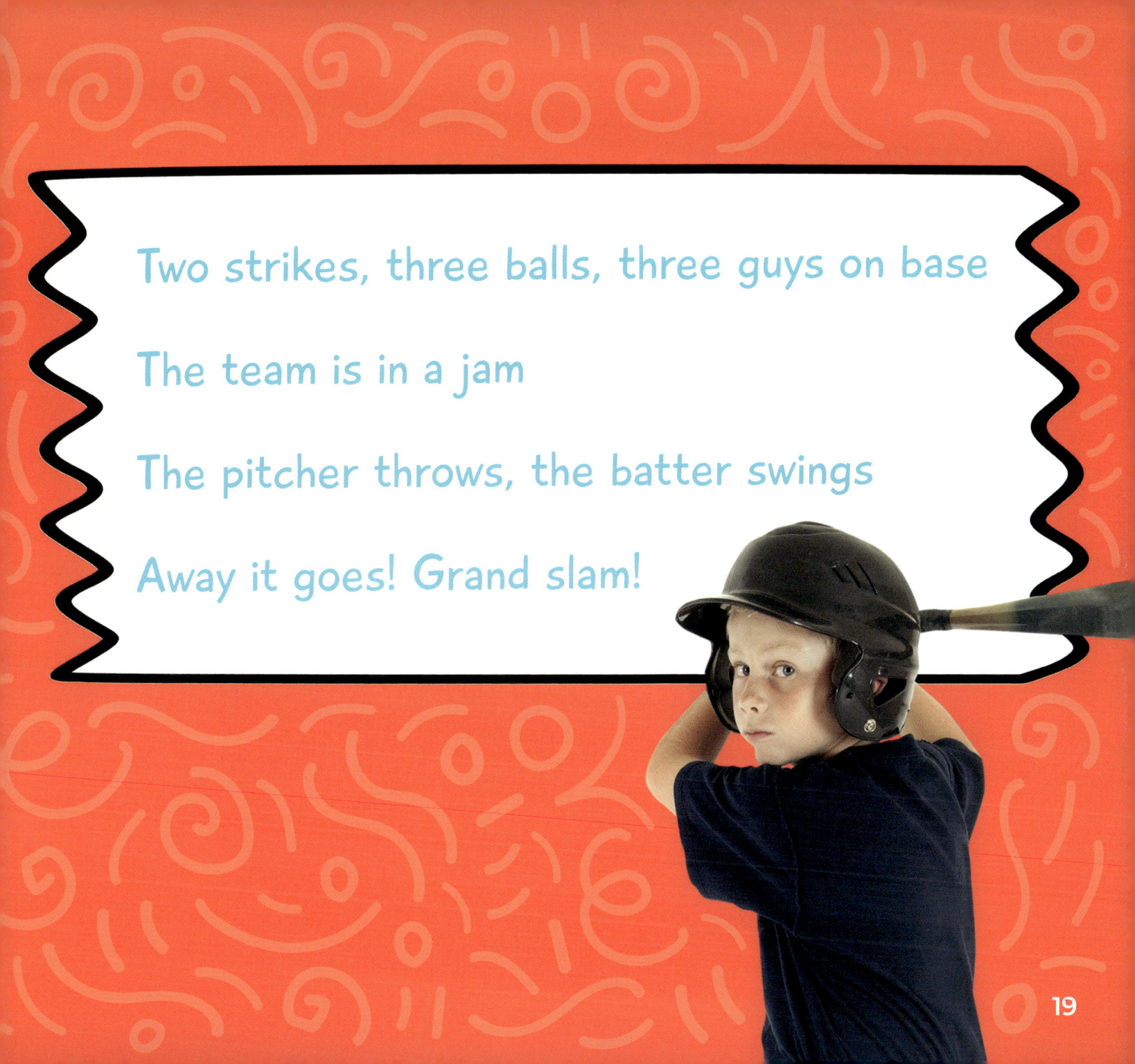

The team is in a jam

The pitcher throws, the batter swings

Away it goes! Grand slam!

FAVORITE THINGS QUATRAINS

Write a quatrain about a favorite thing. This could be a bike, stuffed animal, or other object. Describe the object using your five senses. Write about what the object does. Or describe how it makes you feel.

When playing my guitar

I travel to the stars

And music meets my soul

No matter where I go

CHARACTER QUATRAINS

Use a quatrain to write about a favorite character. Choose a character from a book, TV show, or movie. Think of a cool scene the character was in. Your quatrain can describe this scene. It could also describe a scene you imagine.

You could even write about a character you invent!

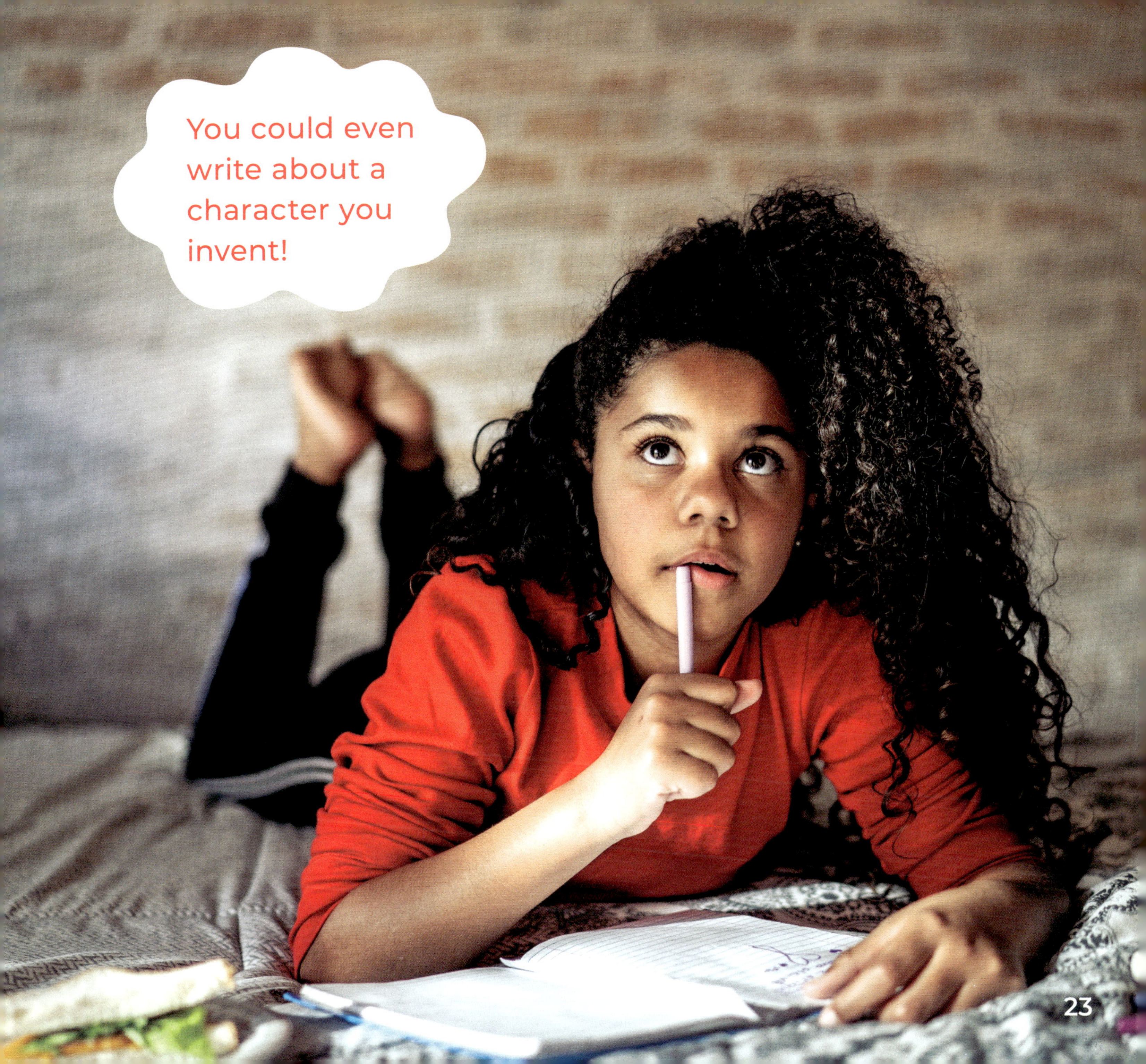

Write down words related to the scene. Name other characters who were there. Think about **emotions** your character felt.

Find **rhymes** for some of these words. Then write some lines describing the scene.

When Humpty Dumpty took a fall

He must have felt quite scared

But all the king's horses and men

Showed him how much they cared

FRIENDSHIP QUATRAINS

Write a quatrain about a friend. Your poem might describe your friend's **traits**. It might be about something you do together. It can also describe how your friendship makes you feel.

My friend Sophia lives next door

She walks with me to school

In summertime we play outside

And swim in lakes and pools

SHARING YOUR QUATRAIN

You can share your poem by reading it aloud. This lets listeners hear the **rhymes**. You can also share your poem online with a parent's permission. Choose a background or photo to go with the poem.

You might also share your poem on a poetry website.

GLOSSARY

emotion (ih-MOH-shuhn)—a state of mind or feeling.

equipment—items needed for a certain activity.

near rhyme—a word that sounds very similar to another but isn't an exact rhyme.

rhyme—to end with the same sound as another word.

rhyme scheme—a pattern for rhyming lines in a poem.

stanza—a group of lines in a poem.

syllable—one of the parts a word is divided into based on the way it is pronounced. A syllable usually contains one vowel sound.

trait—a quality or feature that defines something.

ONLINE RESOURCES

Booklinks
NONFICTION NETWORK
FREE! ONLINE NONFICTION RESOURCES

To learn more about quatrain poems, please visit **abdobooklinks.com** or scan this QR code. These links are routinely monitored and updated to provide the most current information available.

INDEX

action words, 16
animals, 9, 12, 13, 14, 15, 25

characters, 22, 23, 24, 25

Dickinson, Emily, 6, 7, 9

favorite things, 16, 20, 21, 22
feelings, 20, 24, 25, 26
friendship, 26, 27

Khayyam, Omar, 5

lines, 4, 8, 10, 14, 18, 24

Massachusetts, 6

rhyme schemes, 8, 9, 14, 15
rhyming, 8, 9, 12, 14, 15, 18, 24, 28

senses, 20
sharing, 28, 29
sports, 16, 17, 18, 19
stanzas, 4, 6
syllables, 10, 11

3 1333 05237 4731